BLACKBEARD;
OR,
THE PIRATE OF THE ROANOKE.

INSIGHT PUBLICA®

Nadakkavu, Kozhikode, Kerala, 673011
www.insightpublica.com
e-mail: insightpublica@gmail.com
Title: **BLACKBEARD; OR, THE PIRATE OF THE ROANOKE**
Author: **B. BARKER**
First Insight Edition: May 2025
Printed and Published by
InsightinPublica Printers & Publishers Pvt. Ltd.
ISBN: 978-93-5517-539-7
₹ 120

BLACKBEARD;
OR,
THE PIRATE OF THE ROANOKE.

B. BARKER

INSIGHT PUBLICA®

CHAPTER I.

The Island of Trinidad. Landing of the Earl of Derwentwater and his party upon the Isle—Its Enchanted Scenery. Unnatural Sounds. Sudden appearance of the Notorious Pirate Blackbeard.

Situated upon the broad bosom of the vast Atlantic Ocean, about two hundred leagues from the coast of Brazil, is a small but fertile island, which has retained from the period of its first discovery, the familiar name of Trinidad. This beautiful island, although a lovely and sequestered spot, has been for various general reasons, but rarely visited by the hardy mariners of the deep, and never permanently settled or inhabited by man. Its surface is agreeably diversified with high hills and low beautiful valleys, whilst its circumference is almost wholly surrounded by a chain of dark, rocky cliffs, which gives to this remote island a somewhat fantastic appearance to the eye of the beholder, as he approaches it from the sea. On this circumscribed but favored spot of earth, nature seems to have reveled in almost boundless profusion, scattering here and there throughout its valleys her choicest favors, in the shape of delicious tropical fruits, and ever green luxuriant herbage, whose fragrance as it mingled with the pure fresh breeze of the ocean, has proved to be a sweet balsam of health to many a sick and weary mariner as he sailed within reach of its invigorating influence. Although this fair island possessed no convenient harbor for its vessels of any class, still there was upon its southern side, a small piece of white sandy beach, upon which a single boat might easily land, and here upon this same spot, a boat did land about an hour after sunrise, on the thirty-first day of October, 1717.

The boat in question, was occupied by six persons, who, as soon as its keel grazed upon the clear white sand, immediately disembarked and dispersed themselves singly and by twos, in different directions for the purpose of enjoying a short ramble amongst the shady trees and fragrant foliage of the island.

The party to which we have alluded, consisted of the Earl of Derwentwater, a noble looking gentleman, who, apparently had but just spent the prime of life,—his fair niece, Mary Hamilton, a stately and beautiful girl, about twenty-three years of age,—Arthur Huntington and his twin brother, Henry—a huge red headed but fat and good natured son of the 'Emerald Isle,' who acted in the capacity of servant to the earl, and last, though by no means least, a beautiful golden haired, cherry cheerful nymph of fourteen, whom for the sake of a name we shall call Ellen Armstrong.

After having rambled about for a short space of time, the earl and his fair niece suddenly encountered each other on the brow of a rising eminence, when the latter then accosted her companion:

'Dear uncle, this lovely island seems to me, like a miniature paradise, wherein I could always wish to live as long as the precious boon of life should be granted unto me.'

'I declare, Mary,' replied the earl, as a slight smile passed over his noble countenance, 'you appear to be an enthusiast in every thing. I grant, that this is a beautiful spot, yet not to be compared in my estimation, even for a moment, with my lovely park near London, in merry old England.'

'But, you forget, dear uncle,' replied Mary Hamilton, 'that our English parks are not now what they once were.'

'How so, Mary, do not the staunch old oaks, grow to a height as lofty as of yore?'

'Perhaps they do, but still, uncle, there is too much art mixed up with nature, in our English scenery. Here all is nature.'

'And I think you must be a very great lover of it, if you prefer this hilly, iron bound island, to the level green sward of Derwent park,' replied the earl.

'I must still plead guilty of the charge of loving nature as it is, uncle,' responded Mary. 'I have seen it in a great variety of forms. I have viewed its high grandeur amid the forests and mountains of America; but never before this hour, have I ever seen it so pure, so serene, and so calmly beautiful.'

'I must needs own, that this is at present, a quiet place enough,' answered the earl, 'but do you not know, dear Mary, that even here, the face of nature is oft times suddenly changed, by the awful sweep of the howling hurricane, or the thundering shock of the subterraneous earthquake.'

'Why, I really believe, that you are getting to be enthusiastic now, dear uncle,' replied Mary Hamilton, 'but we cannot exactly agree, I move that we drop the subject forthwith.'

'And I second the motion,' laughingly responded the noble earl.—'But look at the ship, Mary, and see, she is almost hull down in the distance.'

The vessel to which the earl alluded, the white sails of which were just visible to his eyes and those of his companion, from the eminence on which they stood, was the honorable East India Company's ship Gladiator, to which belonged the boat that had conveyed the Earl and his party to the shore, in the manner before related. She was bound to Rio Janeiro, from thence to Batavia, and as they had a long passage from the Downs, Captain Rowland was easily persuaded to allow his distinguished passenger the long coveted recreation of visiting the small though beautiful island of Trinidad.

'Rowland is going to make a long tack, this time I guess,' continued the earl, as they both stood watching the still lessening sails of the huge Indiaman.

'Suppose, dear uncle, replied Mary Hamilton, 'that this Captain Rowland should sail away and leave us here upon this remote island.'

'Then you would have a most excellent chance to study nature as it is,' responded the earl playfully. 'But Rowland would never dare to do any such foolish thing as that to which you have alluded.'

'It may be so, uncle, but still I must sincerely confess, that there is something about this Captain Rowland and his general conduct which I by no means like.'

'Oh, you are too fastidious, dear Mary,' replied the earl, 'for I am sure that as far as my observation has gone, Captain Rowland has conducted himself thus far during our voyage, in a very kind and gentlemanly manner.'

'Your observation has not extended as far as mine, uncle, if it had you would have noticed the sardonic and sinister expression of this captain's countenance, as he oft times gazed upon the fair form of sweet Ellen Armstrong.'

'What a suspicious mortal you are, Mary. Why, I would trust Rowland's honor amongst a thousand Ellen Armstrongs, or Mary Hamiltons either.'

'God grant that your trust in his good intentions may be well founded,' replied Mary seriously, then adroitly turning the conversation, she continued, 'see uncle, there is Arthur Huntington and Ellen Armstrong at the bottom of the hill—let us join them.'

Having thus spoken, Mary Hamilton accepted the aid of the earl's proffered arm, and both together leisurely descended the hill, intently gazing upon the sea, they did so as if watching the slow progress of the ship, which was now standing in towards the land.

So very busy was sweet Ellen Armstrong, in catching each enthusiastic word as it fell from the lips of Arthur Huntington, whilst he eloquently descanted on the beauties of the island scenery—she was scarcely aware of the near vicinity of her elder intruders, until Mary Hamilton approached her closely and spoke as follows:

'Oh, Ellen, what a monopolizer you are of the attention of young gentlemen. First, you led Mr. Henry Huntington in a wild goose chase all around the island, and next, we find you holding a very confidential 'tete-a-tete' with young Mr. Arthur. Such proceedings are really too bad, and, as your watchful 'duenna,' I must enter my serious protest against them.'

These words were spoken in a playful bantering kind of manner, which caused the rich red blood to mantle over the face and neck of the beautiful Ellen, whilst she answered in the same tone:

'I humbly crave your pardon, most gracious and prudent 'duenna,' for having been the only one of the party who designed to treat the young gentlemen to whom you have alluded, with ordinary civility.'

'She has you there, Mary,' exclaimed the earl, 'and it is now your turn to blush for not doing the amiable to at least one of the twin brothers.'

Before Mary could find words wherewith to reply to her uncle's bantering speech, a low sweet strain of mournful music, fell suddenly upon the ears of our astonished voyagers, which as it died slowly away, like the departing imagery of a vivid dream, was succeeded instantly by a loud shout of bacchanalian laughter, which echoed wildly for a moment amongst the rocky cliffs of the island, then all was calm and silent as before.

The surprise occasioned by these strange and mysterious sounds, caused the earl and his companions to stand, for some moments after their conclusion in a state of profound and bewildered silence, almost breathlessly listening as if to hear them again repeated. But, they listened in vain, for the strange sounds were no more heard, and the painful silence which had overpowered our singular group of island visitors, was soon after broken by the Earl of Derwentwater, who spoke as follows:

'I really believe, that this place is a sort of mixture, composed of equal portions of fairy land and satan's paradise, judging by the different sounds which we have just heard.'

'The music must have proceeded from a flute,' said Arthur Huntington.

'And it must have been played by a master's hand,' interposed Mary Hamilton.

'I can never believe that those were earthly sounds,' said Ellen Armstrong, 'and I must say for one, I have no wish to remain here longer.'

'You, surely, cannot be already tired of roaming about this lovely spot,' exclaimed Mary Hamilton in a deprecating tone. 'I should have thought, that after complaining as you have of the tediousness and monotony of our sea voyage, you would be the last one to express a wish to leave this beautiful island.'

'I have well appreciated the beauties of this quiet place,' replied Ellen, 'but at the risk of being considered a very weak and simple girl, I must own, that the mysterious sounds which just now fell upon my ears, cannot be accounted for through any natural means, and as I have no particular liking for supernatural adventures, I must persist in my wish to go on board our good ship again, as soon as possible.'

As the fair Ellen finished her speech, light strains of the same mysterious music which they had before heard, again floated through the air above their heads, the same bacchanalian shouts of wild laughter again fell upon their ears, but, as its last strange echo died away, the surprise of our island visitors was greatly augmented by the sudden appearance before them, of a tall and handsomely formed man, effeminately dressed in loose Turkish trousers of crimson silk, which were elegantly matched by a loose tunic of the same color and texture.—This was fastened to his person by a red silken sash, which also confined in its soft but close embrace, a large pair of pistols and a small Spanish stiletto of the most costly workmanship. The head of this strange being was covered with a crimson cap, and his countenance, might have been truely termed handsome, had not the lower part of it been enveloped in a mass of long black hair, which gave to its possessor an air of wild and savage ferocity. (See Engraving.)

'What strange apparition is this,' exclaimed the earl involuntarily, as this singular personage stood erect before him.

'I am no apparition, sir,' exclaimed the stranger, in a voice so finely modulated, that it might have been easily taken for a woman's, 'but a substantial specimen of vigorous life, who kindly bids you welcome to the pirates' palace.'

'And, who, then are you?' exclaimed the undaunted Earl, altering his voice to a deep, rough tone. The stranger smiled sardonically upon the group before him as he answered:

'I am Blackbeard, the far-famed Pirate of the Roanoke!'

Upon hearing these dread words, sweet Ellen Armstrong was obliged to lean tremblingly for support, upon the arm of Arthur Huntington, whilst the stout hearted Earl again addressed the stranger as follows:

'If you are indeed the person whom you have represented yourself to be, learn that I have often heard of your murderous exploits before, and I now call upon you in the name of England's King, to surrender yourself immediately to me, as my prisoner.'

After giving utterance to a loud derisive laugh, whose echo as it reverberated amongst the rocky cliffs, sounded like the fitful mirth of numerous invisible demons, the pirate thus answered the bold summons of the earl.

'You talk boldly for one whose brains I might instantly scatter to the four winds of heaven. Know you not that you and your companions are in my power?'

'I know,' replied the earl, 'that I and my companions by making an easy signal, can soon be supported by an hundred stout hearts from yonder ship, whose—'

'Ha, sayst thou so,' interrupted the stranger, 'I think that they will soon have other business upon their hands. Look yonder.'

CHAPTER II.

Description of Characters. Sweet Ellen Armstrong. Sudden appearance of the Piratical Brig. The Earl's Request. Blackbeard's Decision. The Desperadoes. The decision is enforced. Perilous situation of Mary Hamilton and Ellen.

In order to carry forward the plan of our story in a consistent and intelligible manner, it becomes necessary for us, here, to briefly explain some important particulars relating to the history of the Earl of Derwentwater and his companions, previous to their landing upon the remote Island of Trinidad, as related in the course of our first chapter.

The intelligent reader of history, will undoubtedly recollect, that the year 1715, (two years before the time chosen for the commencement of our romance,) was rendered famous by the important insurrection which then took place throughout England and Scotland, in favor of the Chevalier de St. George, or James the Third, a proud and haughty scion of the Roman Catholic house of Stuart. This singular and renowned rebellion, although premature in its beginning, and short in its duration, caused during its continuence, the Hanoverian incumbent of the English sceptre to tremble for the permanence of his seat on the throne, and though he at first pretended to despise both it and its authors, he was finally compelled to use vigorous and extraordinary means to bring it to a summary and fatal conclusion. Through the instrumentality of foreign troops, and the numerous cabels which sprang up in the rebel camp, King George was soon enabled to quell this Jacobitical insurrection, which otherwise might have proved formidable enough to have overturned the Protestant dynasty of the British realm, and established in its place the despotic hierarchy of the Church of Rome. So well aware was the reigning monarch and his ministers of the truth of the above important fact, that they deemed it imperatively incumbent upon them, in order to deal a death blow to all future attempts of the same nature, to punish all the noblemen and other leading characters connected with it, in the most severe and exemplary manner. Acting upon the above principle, the Privy Council caused immediately to be arrested, about thirty of the Scotch and English nobility, the majority of whom fell by the bloody axe of the executioner, whilst the remainder were sentenced to perpetual banishment.

Amongst this latter class of insurgents, was George Armstrong, Earl of Derwentwater, who succeeded to his father's rank and title, immediately after his decease, which happened somewhere about the year 1694. Some time previous to his death, however, the old earl, through his influence with the crown, had obtained the grant of a large tract of land in the province of South Carolina, near the mouth of the Roanoke river, which was soon after settled by these minor and remote branches of his own extensive family, whose fortunes had become sadly dilapidated by the frequent intestine revolutions which happened in Great Britain during the latter part of the seventeenth century. Upon the accession of Queen Anne to the English throne, the old earl fell into disgrace with the ministry, and with his family retired soon after that event, to his plantations in America. Shortly after his arrival, however, the change of climate proved fatal to his advanced age, and brought on an intermittent fever, which ended his life, and caused his only son, George Armstrong, to succeed to his grand title and extensive estates.

Although the character of the young earl, differed in many important respects from that of his father, still, in one great feature there was an exact resemblance between them. The disposition of the old earl was stubborn, artful and avaricious, whilst that of his son, was frank, open and generous. In temper, the former was cunning, revengeful and unforgiving, whilst that of the latter, though hasty and violent in its outbreaks, would a moment afterwards pass away, leaving no lingering trace of its harsh and cruel effect upon the young earl's strong and vigorous mind. Here, the wide contrast between the characters of the father and son ended,—for the same vaulting ambition which had animated the father, through a long and eventful life, descended upon the son in its full and unstinted measure, whilst in blind and extravagant adherence to the house of Stuart, and the Roman Catholic religion, the son greatly outstripped the father, who had been moderate enough in his political and religious machinations to ensure to him his titles, and cause his estate to remain unconfiscated, and in his own particular keeping.

Instead, however, of copying the temporizing and crafty policy of his father, the young earl, soon after his accession to the title and fortune of the former, began openly to hold a correspondence with the court of the pretender, which finally resulted in his becoming one of the first noblemen to assist in raising the rebel banner in Scotland, in the year 1715. After running through a short career of active service, George Armstrong the last Earl of Derwentwater, found his vast estates confiscated to the crown, and himself a prisoner in the Tower of London. This event happened during the spring of 1716. Early in the summer of the same year, he, with a number of others was brought to trial before a special commission appointed for that purpose, found guilty of high treason, (and although, others who had taken a less active part in the rebellion, were doomed to immediate execution.) The earnest intercession of the French Ambassador at the court of St. George Armstrong, to be commuted to foreign and perpetual banishment, and in accordance with this sentence, he was about to join his brother-in-law, a rich South American merchant, who was located at Rio Janeiro in Brazil, when his progress was somewhat singularly arrested by the adventure commenced in our first chapter.

Having related as much of the earl's previous history, as is consistent with the progress of our story, the next of our voyagers in order of description, is his fair niece, Mary Hamilton. In form, as we have before said, she was stately and beautiful, her features were striking and regular, though they could not be called pre-eminently beautiful, whilst her complexion was fair and elegantly transparent. Her hair, which was as dark in color as the plumage of the raven, as it clustered in short, rich, silken curls over her small white neck, gave conclusive evidence, when combined to a pair of large, languishing black eyes, that she was not born beneath the ruddy influence of England's cold and vacillating climate. And such was the fact, for the mother that bore her was of pure Castilian blood, who had fallen in love with and married William Hamilton, whilst residing with her father, who, at that time, held the high situation of Governor of the Island of Cuba. Under the warm and enervating influences of the climate of this island, Mary Hamilton first saw the light, but long before she had learnt to lisp her mother's name, she was sent to England, there to receive, through the agency of her uncle, an education calculated to fit her for the station she would be called upon to assume, as the only child and heir of the ancient house of Hamilton. As she advanced from infancy to childhood, and her young mind began gradually to expand, nature (that beautiful but mystic chain which connects man with his Creator,) prompted her to ask for her mother. The answer which fell from her aunt's lips, in cold and icy tones, which precluded all farther questioning, was,

'Mary, your maternal parent is dead, but I will be a mother to you so long as I live, and my husband shall be to you an indulgent father. And now, dear Mary,' continued Lady Armstrong, 'for various reasons which cannot now be explained, I must strictly prohibit you from alluding to your real mother in my presence, or that of my husband.'

Many a long and bitter hour as she passed from childhood to youth, and from thence to woman's estate, did the future heiress of the House of Hamilton ponder sadly over the mysterious and cruel prohibition of her noble aunt, and as she thus pondered, a strong but indefinite presentiment of future sorrow and grief and misery in connection with the fate of her real parents became so completely fastened upon her mind as to cause her whole deportment to become tinged with a sort of sad and mournful melancholy, which all the seductive arts of a London life could not eradicate.

Although numberless suitors of almost every variety of rank and character had knelt in real and assumed adoration before the virtuous shrine of the beautiful West Indian heiress, she had turned from them all with almost loathing indifference, and the summons which she received (about three months previous to the commencement of our story) calling upon her to join her father, in company with her uncle, found her at the age of twenty-three, unmarried and unengaged. In less than a month however, after her embarcation on board of the Gladiator, a gradual change had taken place in her whole demeanor, caused by the deep interest she found herself constrained to take in the person of Henry Huntington, the son of Sir Arthur Huntington, who had followed the fortunes of the Earl of Derwentwater during the rebellion, and who had chosen also to share his banishment. The baronet was a fine specimen of the old English cavaliers, who had freely spent the greater portion of a handsome fortune in the service of the Stuart family, and now, when nearly at the close of a long and eventful life, he with his twin sons (whose poor mother had died in giving them birth,) had left their own dear and native soil, to live, and perhaps to die in a foreign land.

These twin sons and brothers, Henry and Arthur Huntington, had arrived (at the time of which we are speaking,) to the age of twenty-two, and in personal appearance they might have been considered as correct models of manly beauty. Their forms were tall, erect, and muscular, and thus far, each was the exact counterpart of the other, but here the resemblance between the brothers ended. In temper and disposition, Henry was mild, generous and forgiving, whilst Arthur was sanguine, violent and irascible. Although they had both been educated alike, they differed very widely in strength of mind and capacity of intellect, for the mind of Henry was strong, and undeviatingly based on the principles of right, while that of his brother was weak and vacillating. The affections of the former when once fixed, were immoveable as the solid rock, whilst the passions of the latter, although more violent, were not capable of remaining fixed for any length of time on any particular object. These two brothers had both felt a partiality for Mary Hamilton, and so far as Henry was concerned, the partiality was fully reciprocated, but she looked coldly upon Arthur, which caused him to turn from her in disgust, and transport his vacillating affections to sweet Ellen Armstrong, whom, as being our principal heroine, we must now proceed briefly to notice and describe.

At the time of her introduction to the notice of our readers, she was to all outward appearance a bright and joyous being, who seemed to think of nothing but the happiness of herself and those around her. Although but fourteen summers had then passed over her head, and her fair form was slight and fragile as the first pale flower of Spring, her high and noble thoughts, as they escaped from her vermillion lips in soft and musical words, gave sufficient evidence that her mind and intellect was far beyond her years. She was, in very fact and deed, a singular and uncommon being, such an one as is rarely to be met with in the daily walks of life. Her form, though slight, was faultless in its proportions, her countenance was intelligent and highly expressive, whilst in her fair complexion, the pure red and white, seemed to have been most judiciously combined. To all these embellishments, permit us to add, a head of luxuriant hair, of a golden auburn color, with a pair of large and sparkling blue eyes, shaded by long, dark, silken eye lashes, and the personal portrait of our heroine is complete. Her character, also, in many of its traits was as good as her person was beautiful. The bland sweetness of her disposition and the apparent mildness of her temper, had even in the years of her childhood, endeared her to all who happened to be within reach of her acquaintance, but still she had faults, for there are none perfect, no, not one. Ellen Armstrong was fanciful, wayward, and highly romantic, a being of strong and ardent passions which would sometimes, in spite of the watchful vigilance which she always endeavored to keep over them, get the better of her right judgment, and high sense of rectitude.

Presuming, kind reader, that you may have inferred that sweet Ellen Armstrong, as the Earl was wont to term her, was his daughter, we must now undeceive you, stating that such was not the case. The history of her connection with the earl was as follows:

As he returned home from an exciting session of the House of Peers, late on a cold night in December, 1703, (nearly 14 years previous to the date of the commencement of our story,) he was greatly surprised, upon entering the drawing-room of his elegant mansion, to find his wife busily employed in fondling and carressing a beautiful infant, apparently not more than two or three weeks old.

'What does this all mean, Lady Armstrong?' exclaimed the earl, as soon as his surprise had in a measure subsided.

'Listen, and I will tell you,' replied the lady, 'About two hours ago, the street-door bell rang violently, which caused me to despatch a serving maid to ascertain from whom this loud summons proceeded. She immediately went to the door and opened it, but found no one there. Upon turning back again into the entry, her ears were assailed by the faint cries of this dear babe, whom she soon after discovered, esconced very comfortably in a large wicker basket. This with its contents was soon conveyed to my presence, and upon removing the infant from its place of rest, I found this note attached to its dress.'

So saying, Lady Armstrong handed a letter to her husband, which he opened, and then read from it as follows:

'To the Right Honorable George Armstrong, Earl of Derwentwater.

Sir: The writer of this, being well aware that your matrimonial union still remains unblest with children, would earnestly entreat you to adopt the infant which this accompanies, as your own. If you should see fit to comply with my request, you can rest assured that no pecuniary means shall be wanting, to insure to her, if she lives, all the educational and other accomplishments fitting to your rank, and that to which at some future day she herself, will be entitled. A draft for the necessary funds will be punctually placed at your disposal at the commencement of each year, until those who have a right, shall claim her at your hands. If you do right by her, you will gain the approval of a good conscience; if not, you will feel the vengeance of a parent's heart. But I can explain no farther. Adieu, yours, &c.,

'MONTMORENCI.'

After having read the above singular epistle, the earl

held a long consultation with his amiable wife, which resulted in their concluding to comply with the request of the mysterious writer, to adopt the poor foundling as their own daughter, and at the same time, they determined never to reveal to her the secret of her strange advent amongst them. In accordance with these resolutions a suitable nurse for the young infant was immediately procured, and when it had reached a proper age, it was baptized by the name of Ellen Armstrong.

Such kind readers, is a brief description of the person and fortunes of our heroine, previous to the commencement of our narrative, and now presuming your generous permission as granted, we shall now proceed to extend the great chain of events connected with our singular and romantic history.

As the pirate Blackbeard, uttered in a commanding tone the words recorded at the close of our first chapter, he pointed with his finger towards the ship, and as the earl involuntarily turned his eyes in the same direction, he observed a small brig then about two miles off, making all sail towards the island, which caused him to say, in answer to the pirate's words:

'I have looked yonder as you directed me to do, yet I can see nothing but our own noble ship, and another vessel which appears to be a much smaller one.'

'If you will have the goodness to look again,' replied Blackbeard, somewhat satirically, 'you will see that the small vessel gains very fast upon the larger one.'

'There seems to be nothing very strange or alarming about that,' answered the earl.

'You may possibly, soon have occasion to entertain a very different opinion.'

'How so?' asked the earl.

'Because the small vessel appears to be a piratical brig,

whose commander, I am well assured, will not pass a rich Indiaman without politely undertaking to inspect his inventory and overhaul his cargo,' replied the pirate.

'I am rather inclined to think,' answered the earl, 'that he will first be favored through the medium of our guns with an opportunity to cultivate an extensive acquaintance with the sharks and other monsters of the deep. Now, sir,' he continued, turning to the pirate, 'we will with your leave, get as quickly as possible on board of our own ship.'

'Oh, certainly,' replied Blackbeard, 'only, as it appears to me quite probable, that these two young ladies will be exposed to great danger in getting on board of your noble ship, I shall claim the privilege of keeping them here under my protection until I learn the result of the engagement, which I am sure the piratical commander of the brig is about to venture upon.'

As the pirate calmly concluded his strange speech, sweet Ellen Armstrong sank fainting into the arms of Arthur Huntington; and Mary Hamilton, with a blanched cheek, shrank closer to her uncle's side, as he thus indignantly addressed the pirate:

'Villain, I command you to leave the presence of these ladies, instantly.'

'Until their safety is duly cared for, I shall not stir from this spot,' coolly replied the pirate.

'Take your fair burthen to the boat, Arthur,' exclaimed the earl, impatiently, 'and I will follow you.'

'You may go, but the ladies will remain,' said the pirate decidedly, who at the same time gave a loud peculiar whistle, and the next moment the earl found himself and his companions surrounded by a band of ferocious desperadoes, who, with brandished weapons, stood ready to execute the commands of their leader.

'Two of you take these ladies to the palace,' exclaimed

Blackbeard, 'whilst the remainder of you will see the gentlemen safely embarked for yonder ship.'

Although the earl and Arthur Huntington resisted manfully, their efforts were unavailing, for whilst the two ladies were borne off in one direction, they were quickly hurried on board their boat and compelled by the threats of their ruffianly assailants to row swiftly towards the noble Gladiator.

CHAPTER III.

Mary Hamilton and Ellen Armstrong Captured and conveyed to the Pirate Palace. Contemplated Escape—Frustrated by Blackbeard. Ellen afterwards conveyed on board the Pirate Brig.

In spite of their entreaties, the females were ruthlessly torn away from their companions, and conducted by these remorseless ruffians to the pirate's palace. Mary then thought, that the beauty and loveliness of the island, which, but a few hours previous she would not have exchanged for all England, she would now gladly quit for the meanest spot on Briton's Isle.

Sweet Ellen murmured to herself that the horrible forebodings she had in reference to the island, were but the precursor of what might be expected. The grandeur and sublimity of its scenery, its isolated position, being surrounded by the waters of the Atlantic—the unnatural music and noises, all conspired to fill the mind of this young girl with the idea that something was about to transpire of no ordinary nature,—and neither was she deceived.

A great change however, had been wrought in the course of the last few hours, upon the thoughts and feelings of our two fair captives, a change which had caused reality to usurp for a time at least, the place of romance, and constrained them to gaze with a vacant look upon the superbly natural beauties of the island glen. Therefore with thoughts concentrated upon their immediate personal prospects and fruitless conjectures as to the complexion of their coming fate, the fair captives mechanically followed the footsteps of their guides, who when they had reached the bottom of the hill, suddenly stopped before the open door of a long building which had been ingeniously constructed of bamboo and other light materials well suited for the covering of a cool place of shelter, under the heat of a tropical sun. There was nothing farther, worthy of remark about its exterior appearance, with the exception of its being so thickly covered on all sides by the luxuriant and evergreen foliage of the surrounding trees, as to preclude it from being seen from the tops of the adjacent hills, but its interior contained four large apartments, two of which had been fitted up in a manner luxurious, and even elegant.

Into one of these two rooms, whose walls were decorated and hung round with the richest crimson drapery, and which was as richly furnished in every other respect, did the strange guides usher their fair prisoners, after which, they instantly retired, leaving our heroine and her companion to consult together as they might see fit upon their singular and mysterious situation.

'Do we dream dear Mary,' exclaimed Ellen, us she gazed wildly around this strange apartment, 'or are we laboring under the influence of some fairy spell of necromantic enchantment?'

'Would to Heaven, that it was so,' exclaimed Mary, in reply, 'but alas, it is not. For the present at least, dear Ellen, we are in the power of ferocious pirates, from whom, I hope we shall soon be released.'

'How?' asked Ellen, hardly realizing what she said.

'Through the agency of our friends on ship-board' replied Mary.

'Oh yes, I recollect now,' said Ellen. 'My father and Arthur have gone on board our vessel, but I have seen nothing of Henry or Patrick, since we first landed upon this fatal spot. Where do you think they can be?'

'I have been trying to convince my mind of their safety, ever since we fell in with our cruel captors,' answered Mary, 'yet I cannot say that I have succeeded in so doing. From the top of some adjacent hill, they may have witnessed the scenes which transpired on the occasion of our capture, and concealed themselves in some of the fissures of the rocky cliffs, there to await assistance from the ship, or—'

'They may have been taken prisoners, by the pirates, as you call them,' interrupted Ellen.

'Heaven forbid,' exclaimed Mary earnestly. 'But if that should be the fact,' continued the fair girl, after a moment's pause, 'I feel greatly consoled by the hope that they, as well as ourselves, will find a speedy release from this horrible bondage.'

'I'm sure it will not be Captain Rowland's fault, if we are not very soon liberated,' replied Ellen.

'You seem to be rather partial towards this Captain Rowland,' Mary carelessly remarked.

'Partial, what mean you by that, Mary?' asked Ellen, as a slight blush overspread her beautiful features. 'He has been very kind and attentive to all of us during our voyage, and such treatment requires, in my opinion, at least civility in return.'

Before Mary could find time to reply to the words of her companion, the ears of both our fair captives were suddenly astonished by the sound of a female voice, singing in a sweet, low tone of touching melody the following words—

'Beware, beware,

Of the false and fair,

For many a noble form,
Hides a heart within,
Quite as full of sin,
And as black as the midnight storm.'

'This must be the very palace of enchantment,' exclaimed Ellen, as the voice of the singer abruptly ceased, 'where one could almost be led to forget their own personal identity. But hark, I hear the strange voice again.'

Ellen and her companion again listened in almost breathless silence as the invisible vocalist continued her song, thus:

'Beware, beware,
For grief and care
Broods over the youthful heart,
And the chastening rod
Of an Infinite God,
His justice will soon impart.'

Here the voice of the invisible songster again ceased, and although both Ellen and her companion listened long for its repetition, they listened in vain, for it was heard no more.

After a short interval of silence had elapsed, Mary Hamilton addressed her companion as follows—

'The thought has just entered my mind of attempting to escape from this strange and horrible place.'

'I must own, dear Mary,' replied Ellen, 'that the place is strange enough to terrify a less romantic person than myself, still I think it far from being horrible. This room is almost as elegantly furnished as was my dear mother's in London, and then only think of the delightful music which has so lately greeted our ears.'

'Think too, of the horrid farce we have seen,' continued

Mary.—'Earnestly consider, dear Ellen, that we are in the power of pirates and murderers, whose motives for detaining us, cannot be any thing but evil, and then say if you will join me in making an attempt to escape.'

'You talk of escaping from the pirate's palace, as though it were the most easy and practicable thing in the world,' exclaimed Blackbeard, who had abruptly entered the apartment from an inner room, and had stood unperceived behind the captives whilst Mary Hamilton had spoken the words quoted above.

Startled by the sudden and unexpected appearance of their strange, yet famous captor, our two maidens were at first awed into silence, but it was of short duration, for Mary Hamilton quickly gathered sufficient courage to enable her to answer the pirate's words as follows:

'If it is not an easy thing for us to escape, surely you possess the power to make it so.'

'True, I possess the power,' replied the pirate, somewhat ironically, 'yet for the present at least, I lack the inclination. So you must make yourselves as contented as you can here in my poor house, until I can make arrangements for your future government.'

'Allow me to ask, sir, by what right it is that you, a person totally unknown to us, have forcibly abducted from their natural protectors, two poor females who never harmed you nor yours?'

'Believe me, Miss Hamilton,' answered the pirate earnestly, 'when I tell you that I have not acted in the manner of which you speak, without reason. But my motives and reasons, I shall take the liberty of explaining when and where I please.'

'Were your motives such as would do honor to an angel,' replied Mary, 'it would not alter my opinion either of yourself or your actions. I believe you to be both a pirate, and murderer, and—'

'Stop, you have said enough,' exclaimed Blackbeard, sternly. 'If you do not fear the consequences of such rash speaking for yourself, know that I hold in my hand the power of life and death over thy betrothed lover.'

'My worst forebodings are then realized,' exclaimed Mary in a faltering tone, 'and I must condescend to sue for mercy at your feet.—Mercy, not for myself, but for him who is far dearer to me than life.'

'He is almost too dangerous a character to receive clemency at my hands,' answered the pirate, 'for his capture and that of his servant, has cost one of the bravest of my crew his life, therefore, according to our code of laws, which require blood for blood, he is answerable to immediate death. But the pardoning power still remains in my hands, and I am willing to spare him upon one condition.'

'Name, oh name it,' exclaimed Mary, eagerly.

'It is this,' continued the pirate. 'You must consent to marry Captain Rowland.'

As these dread words fell into accents cold and calm upon her ears, the self possession which had distinguished her throughout the foregoing conversation, suddenly passed away, and poor Mary Hamilton sunk utterly bereft of consciousness upon one of the richly cushioned seats which ornamented the apartment, while sweet Ellen Armstrong almost as terrified as her companion, looked vacantly around, and as if not comprehending the import of the pirate's significant speech.

After gazing fixedly for a few moments upon the forms of the two fair creatures before him, Blackbeard stepped softly to the door from which he had made his ingress into the apartment, and in a low but distinct voice uttered the following words:

'Violette, come hither.'

A moment or two of dead silence intervened, and then a dark complectioned but beautifully formed female entered the apartment, and stood before the pirate, who thus addressed her:

'Seest thou, Violette, that lady reclining upon yonder seat, with face as pale as death?'

Casting her eyes in the direction intimated by the pirate's glance, she gave a nod of assent as he continued:

'I am about to leave this place for a short season, and in the meanwhile I wish to place this fair lady in your keeping.'

'And her companion also?' asked Violette.

'No; she accompanies me.'

'It is well,' replied Violette, 'your orders shall be faithfully obeyed.'

The pirate here whispered a few words in the ear of the dark female, who immediately after approached the seat where Mary was reclining, stamped thrice with her tiny foot upon the floor, when two hideous looking negressess entered the apartment, and at a sign from Violette, they instantly removed the still prostrate form of Mary Hamilton into the inner room.

This last singular and unnatural proceeding totally confused the few ideas which had remained to poor Ellen after her friend had swooned, and as the loud booming of distant cannon fell upon her ear, she too would have sank fainting to the floor, had not Violette sprang forward and caught her in her arms.

CHAPTER IV.

Marine Phraseology. Approach of the Piratical Brig. History of Captain Rowland. A Conflict expected. A Boat from the Shore. The Ship Surrenders. Sudden appearance of Blackbeard and Ellen Armstrong on board of the Brig. Heroic Conduct of Arthur Huntington. Ellen steps between him and Death. The Result. Ellen in Despair.

'Mast-head, there!'

'Halloo.'

'Keep a sharp look-out there for a sail.'

'Aye, aye, sir.'

The above short but professional dialogue took place between Captain Roderick Rowland, of the good ship Gladiator, and his third officer, (a Mr. Summers by name,) who had been sent to the main-top gallant mast-head immediately after the Earl of Derwentwater and his companions had left the vessel, with the single order, at first, to keep a sharp look-out for the many rocks and reefs which surrounded the island, but Summers had not assumed his station for many minutes before he was peremptorily ordered, (as we have above recorded,) to look out for sails as well as for rocks, which caused the sailor who stood upon the other end of the cross-trees, and who was on regular mast-head duty, thus to address the third officer,—

'Do you suppose, Mr. Summers, that our captain really expects to fall in with a sail in this out-o'-the-way kind of spot?'

'Of course he does,' replied Summers, 'or he wouldn't have told me to look out for one. But why shouldn't a sail be seen here, Bill, as well as anywhere else?'

'Well, I can't exactly say, sir,' answered Bill, (who, by the way, was a fine specimen of a rough and rugged old tar,) 'but I have understood that ships in general have of late years given this little bit of an island a wide berth.'

'Did ever you hear the reason why?' asked Summers.

'Yes, sir, more than forty times, and if my watch wasn't almost out I could spin you a yarn as long as our main-top bowline about the "reason," as you call it.'

Smiling at the seriousness with which the old tar had spoken, the officer replied,

'O never mind the yarn now, Bill, nor the reason either, but look sharp there, about three points off our bow, and see if you cannot catch a glimpse of something high and white, like a sail: I believe I can.'

'And so can I, too, sir,' exclaimed Bill, after having looked for a few moments in the direction intimated.

'It's a strange sail, then, sure enough,' answered the third officer.

'There's no mistake about that, sir,' replied Bill. 'What do you make her out to be, sir?'

'I should take her to be a full rigged brig,' answered Summers.

'So should I,' rejoined the sailor. 'She has got studding sails out a-low and aloft, and appears to be coming up with us hand over fist. Shall I sing out to the captain, sir?'

'No—I will myself. On deck, there!'

'Halloo; what do you see?' answered the captain.

'A full rigged brig, sir.'

'Where away?'

'Three points off our weather-bow.'

'How does she appear to be heading?'

'Direct for us, sir,' was the answer, and as it reached the ears of the captain, he turned to the first officer, who stood beside him, and said—

'Mr. Howe, that strange vessel must be a pirate.'

'What makes you think so, sir?' asked the first lieutenant.

'Because,' replied the Captain, 'if she was anything else she would not be steering directly for us with studding-sails set.'

'Perhaps it may be some vessel in distress,' suggested the lieutenant.

'That may be the case, though I doubt it much,' answered the captain, abruptly, 'but, as I do not wish to create a premature and unnecessary alarm amongst the passengers, we will put the ship on the opposite tack, and then if this stranger is in distress he will show a signal.'

In accordance with the above decision of her commander, the Gladiator, which had been previously standing off from the land, was, (to use a nautical phrase,) immediately put about, which caused her to head in towards the land, and this movement brought the strange brig on the weather quarter, or nearly astern of the ship, and also made her visible to the first lieutenant, who stood eagerly watching for her appearance, on the Gladiator's deck. As soon as he felt sure that his eyes had not deceived him, he said, addressing the captain,

'There she is, sir.'

'Where?' exclaimed Rowland, eagerly, snatching his

spy-glass from its place in the cabin gangway.

'She is in plain sight, sir,' answered the lieutenant, about one point off our weather-quarter.'

'Ah, I see her,' exclaimed the captain after he had looked for a moment through his spy-glass in the direction intimated.

'Does she show any signal, sir?'

'She does not,' replied Rowland, 'and I am convinced she is a piratical vessel. Therefore, Mr. Howe, you will see the ship instantly cleared for action.'

Whilst this last order of the captain was in progress of execution, Rowland, spy-glass in hand, ascended the mizzen rigging of the ship, and kept his eyes intently fixed upon the brig, thus soliloquising as he did so:—

'It is rather a delicate, not to say desperate game, which I have undertaken to play, though so far I have the vanity to think that I have acted my part to admiration. By the most consummate art and address I managed to gain the command of this noble ship, and no one on board, as far as I can learn, has the least suspicion of the manner in which I intend to dispose of her. So far, so good. Now as we are pretty snug in with the land, I will take a look in that direction and see if I can discover what measures are in progress on shore.'

So saying he adjusted his glass to his right eye and turned his gaze towards that part of the island on which the earl and his companions had landed, and after having looked attentively for a few moments in that direction, he exclaimed, whilst a smile of exultation passed across his features,

'Ah, Rowland, you're a deep one, and a fortunate one, too. Every thing connected with your plans seems to prosper, on land as well as sea. Blackbeard has proved himself a good assistant, too, for I can see that he has taken good care of the young ladies, whilst at the same time I perceive that he is about to send the gentlemen back again to their old quarters. I must wear ship, I suppose, and take them on board.' 'On deck, there!'

'Aye, aye, sir,' answered the first lieutenant.

'Put the ship upon the other tack, and brace the head-yards sharp up, leaving the main and main top-sail yards square.'

After this last order had been duly and promptly complied with Captain Rowland descended quickly to the deck, upon reaching which, was thus addressed by his first officer:—

'See, sir, how fast that strange brig gains upon us.'

'I see she does,' answered Rowland, 'and I am sorry that we are obliged to lay aback here, when we should be trying to get the weather-gauge of her. But there is no help for it, for I observe that the earl and his companions have left the shore, and they are now pulling for dear life in order to reach us in time.'

Leaving for the present, the noble Gladiator, with her decks clear for action, and her brave crew awaiting in eager silence, the nearer approach of the piratical vessel, we will proceed to give our readers as much information of the previous character of Captain Roderick Rowland, as is consistent with the present condition and future progress of the scenes of our story, in some of which he is destined to act a conspicuous part.

Descended of wealthy, honorable, and respectable parents, who resided at the time of his birth, (which event happened some forty years before the commencement of our story,) young Rowland, gave during his boyhood such evidences of extraordinary natural capabilities, and superior intellectual capacity, as led those who were connected and acquainted with him to suppose that he might, at some future day, rise to a high rank in the British navy, for which service he seemed to have an unconquerable predilection, and which he entered as midshipman at the age of sixteen. Then it was that his true character began to develope itself, so that during his first cruise, its natural deformity became so apparent as to cause the rest of the officers to look with fear and astonishment upon one, in whom the gifts of extraordinary talents seemed to have been lavished, only to become blended with cunning, artfulness and licentious profligacy, whose disposition was mean and avaricious, and whose temper, though not violent, was cruel, revengeful and unforgiving.

Although young Rowland was also a complete master of the art of dissimulation he did not deem it worth his while to exercise it among the young gentleman of his mess, and he had been but a short time on board His Majesty's ship Vixen, before he was very much feared, and very cordially hated by his equals, whilst he was looked upon with uneasiness and disgust by his superiors.

All these things combined together, rendered Rowland's situation anything but agreeable; so after having been a twelvemonth in the service, he very abruptly left it by taking, what is vulgarly called, a 'French leave' of the Vixen and her officers, whilst that vessel was taking in provisions and water at the island of Madagascar. Here, Rowland, at the age of eighteen, soon fell in with a gang of American and English bucaniers, who, some years previous to that time, had pitched upon this island as a convenient rendezvous to which they might be easily able to repair for recruits and recreation after having, (as they often did,) successfully robbed the rich homeward bound East Indiamen, for whom they usually laid in wait near the pitch of the Cape of Good Hope.

It required but very little persuasion on the part of the pirates to induce one to join them, whose spirit was congenial with theirs, so he very soon became one of the most active and daring of their number. Courage, cunning and cruelty were considered by them to be the most important qualifications of a bona-fide bucanier, and they soon found that these were possessed by Rowland, in a most superlative degree, and this added to the influence of his talents and early education, caused him to rise rapidly to a station of command among them. As it was his motto 'to make hay while the sun shines,' he sailed as soon as possible from Madagascar, from which he had not been absent but twenty days when he fell in with and captured a Spanish Galleon, bound from Genoa to Lisbon, laden with a large amount of gold and silver ornaments, which was the property of the church, and was under the care of a number of ecclesiastics who had taken passage in the unfortunate vessel.

There were a number of other passengers on board, amongst whom was Don Fernando Herrera, who was accompanied by his daughter a beautiful Castilian maiden, then about seventeen years of age, who doated upon her father with all the fondness of a pure and filial affection.

As Rowland acted almost invariably on the principle that dead men tell no tales, he caused all the passengers to be put to death, in detail, until it came the turn of Herrera. As he was about to be cast into the sea, his daughter sprang wildly forward, and kneeling before the cruel pirate captain, she beseeched him in such earnest and pathetic tones to spare her father's life, or let her die in his stead, that Rowland, fired by the voluptuousness of her extreme beauty, and perhaps touched by her tears, promised to spare her father on condition that she would become his wife. Such were the dread alternatives. Death for her father and herself on one hand, and the sacrifice forever of her happiness and peace of mind on the other. In the extremity of her terror, Clarice, (for that was her name,) chose the latter, and that very same night she was united to Rowland, by her own priest and confessor who was compelled to officiate in the ceremony, and her father was compelled to will all of his vast riches in the event of his death to his murderous son-in-law. After having taken to himself a wife in the above strange and summary manner, Rowland repaired to the West Indies, where his father-in-law died soon after his arrival, leaving to the pirate, a vast amount of money and other property, which enabled him to establish himself at Havana, in a most splendid and magnificent manner. His inordinate desire for wealth however still remained unsatiated, and although he left off all open communication with his former associates, (the bucaniers,) still he secretly patronized them, and in return was made acquainted with the result of all their efforts and received a goodly share of their plunder.

Three years had passed away, and Clarice in the interim had presented her husband a boy, but by this time the Spanish authorities had got wind of the manner in which Rowland had obtained his riches, and he was forced to leave Havana, and most of his vast property at the same time, and sail clandestinely and under an assumed name for England. Here he took up his residence in an obscure street of the metropolis where after the expiration of two years, Clarice gave birth to a daughter, whilst relentless death hovered over the fair form of the mother, and soon after removed her gently from the sin and sorrows of a wicked world.

Soon after the decease of his wife, Rowland suddenly left England, but he returned again about a year previous to the commencement of our story, and managed, through sundry letters of recommendation which he himself had forged, to gain the command of the Gladiator.

Leaving the intervening events of his life to become elucidated in the further progress of our story, we will here put an end to our long but important digression and return again to the unravelling of its main thread, by transporting the attention of our readers once more to the deck of Rowland's noble ship.

Here every one was at his station, every thing in its right place, and every soul on board the Gladiator was almost breathlessly watching the near approach of the piratical brig, as, with the horrid black flag flying from her main royal truck, she came sailing majestically down upon the ship, and it was expected by the crew of the latter that an instant combat between the two vessels was inevitable.

Judge then, kind reader, of their supreme astonishment and indignation when they heard the captain, (as the brig fired a couple of blank cartridges across his bows as a signal for him to surrender,) give the following order:

'Mr. Howe, haul down the colors! immediately.'

Instead of jumping immediately, as was generally his wont to obey Rowland's orders, the first lieutenant stood perfectly still, regarding the captain with a puzzled and undecided manner, as much as to ask if he had rightly understood the purport of his superior's words.

'Haul down the colors!' exclaimed the captain the second time, and as he spoke in a stern, loud tone of voice, which precluded all misunderstanding, the first lieutenant, for the first time ventured an answer in the following words:

'Captain Rowland, I must own that I am at a loss to perceive the necessity of hauling down our colors, when we have twice the number of guns possessed by the brig, which would, in case of a conflict, enable us easily to save the ship as well as our own lives.'

'I believe this ship is under my command and not yours, Mr. Howe,' replied Rowland, coolly, 'and I alone am responsible for her safety. Again, sir, I order you to haul down the colors.'

There was something in the cold, calm, passionless manner of Rowland, which awed the lieutenant into compliance, notwithstanding he was naturally a brave man, and he therefore walked forward and repeated to one of the men the captain's order, which a moment afterwards was sullenly obeyed, then a shout of exultation rose up from the crew of the piratical brig, whilst a gun was fired in triumph as her commander prepared to board the ship which had been so ingloriously placed without a struggle within his grasp.

By the time the boat was lowered from the brig, she had ranged up so near the side of the ship, as rendered easy to distinguish from the deck of each the countenances of those on board the other, and as the Earl of Derwentwater and Arthur Huntington, (who had boarded the ship almost unperceived at the time of her surrender,) gazed upon the dark swarthy forms which crowded the sides of the brig, the former suddenly exclaimed—

'Gracious Heaven, Arthur,—yonder on that strange vessel's deck stands Ellen Armstrong with that villain who calls himself the Pirate of the Roanoke close by her side.'

'It cannot be,—where is she?' exclaimed Arthur, involuntarily. 'Thank God, I see her,' he exclaimed, after gazing a moment upon the brig's deck. Another minute elapsed and he was in the water, before any one could anticipate, much less prevent his movements, making towards the piratical brig, which, (as he was an excellent swimmer,) he managed to reach, and he soon found himself by the side of sweet Ellen Armstrong whom he thus addressed:

'Good God! Ellen, how came you here!'

'Arthur!' exclaimed Ellen, faintly,—but she said no more, though Blackbeard answered his query as follows:

'What rashness, young man, caused you to come here?'

'I have come here,' replied Arthur, 'with all the calmness of desperation, to rescue this young lady or die in the attempt.'

'What an uncommonly heroic young gentleman you must be,' responded Blackbeard, satirically, 'to attempt unarmed, and single-handed, the rescue of a young girl from the midst of a hundred armed men. You must certainly be either moon-struck or love-cracked.'

'And you must be a cold-blooded, heartless villain,' exclaimed Arthur, irritated beyond endurance at the scorching irony of the pirate's tone.

'Those are words, young man, which only your life-blood can atone for,' exclaimed the pirate, as he drew a pistol from his belt, and presented it to the young man's breast. 'Die, upstart, die!'

'Rather let me die,' exclaimed sweet Ellen Armstrong, as, quicker than thought, she sprang between the murderous weapon and Arthur's person.

The pirate fired, but the ball did not take effect, and was about to present his second pistol, when he suddenly stopped, and thus addressed a portion of his comrades, who had in meantime gathered round this strange scene.

'Some of you take these two fools below, and confine them in separate apartments until I can attend to the hanging of them.'

Immediately upon the reception of this order, Ellen was dragged by the rough hands of two piratical officers into the brig's cabin, where she was locked up in a small state room, whilst Arthur Huntington, was heavily ironed and confined in the steerage. As the fair Ellen sat in her narrow prison, brooding in mute despair over the horrid scenes she had just passed through, she covered her face with her hands and faintly murmured,

'If Arthur dies, I cannot survive him.'

CHAPTER V.

Henry Huntington and Pat O'Leary, the Earl's Servant, start upon An Exploring Expedition—Its Strange and Sudden Termination at the Pirates' Cavern.

With a love of adventure, which no sense of anticipated or real danger could restrain, glowing upon his mind, and beaming forth from his handsome eyes, did Henry Huntington, upon his first landing upon the island, declare to his companions that he intended to pass the day in exploring its beautiful though limited dimensions, and when hunting for curious sea-shells and other marine curiosities, wherewith to enrich a sort of miniature museum which he had commenced some years before in merry England.

'Is that your real intention, Henry, or are you joking,' asked the earl, as the young man finished speaking.

'I certainly intend, sir, to spend the time allotted to me here, in doing as I have said,' replied Henry.

'Then it is my opinion that you will have a tiresome time of it,' said the earl.

'With all deference to your better judgment, my lord, I anticipate a far different result.'

'Well, then, I wish you all prosperity in your adventurous undertaking,' replied the earl, 'but be careful to keep within sight of the ship.'

'I shall undoubtedly be very careful about that, sir, for although I own that I am an enthusiastic lover of romantic adventures, I do not by any means, aspire to the envious celebrity of being left alone, in all my glory, upon a desolate island. But who amongst all the party is hardy enough to volunteer to go with me. Will you, Arthur?'

'Why, what a selfish fellow you have got to be, Henry,' said Mary Hamilton, 'to start on a wild goose chase yourself, and then ask the only other young gentleman of the party to accompany you.'

'That would be ungallant, without dispute,' chimed in 'sweet' Ellen Armstrong.

'Upon a second thought, I am compelled to believe it would,' replied Henry. 'But to settle the matter, by Lord Armstrong's leave, I will take his servant Patrick with me.'

'Do you hear that, Patrick,' asked the earl?

'Indade, sir, and I do,' replied Mr. Patrick O'Leary, with the true Hibernian accent. 'And its to the end of the world that I would follow swate master Henry, intirely.'

'Well, Patrick, let us take a start now, then,' said Henry.

'Stop a bit, if ye plase, master Henry, till I ask yer honor a bit of a question. Is there any wild bastes on this elligant little island?'

'Not that I know of. But what made you think of that, Patrick?'

'Faith, an it was just this, then, your honor. Ould Father McGrave, rest to his sowl, who was the parish praste at Bully Bannon, when I was a wee bit spalpeen of a boy, used to tell me that in 'forrin' places like this, where the sun was as hot as purgatory all the year round, there was a great plinty of tigers and illifonts, [meaning probably—elephants,] and sarpints, and all other kinds of savage bastes. Now I jest thought, master Henry, if that was the case here, I would just cut a couple of "shillalahs," one for each of us, off of yonder tree, as they might work in handy in case of accidint.'

'Although there is no danger of our being attacked by wild bastes, as you call them,' replied Henry, smiling at the simplicity of the honest Patlander, 'still, the shillalahs may not come amiss, so make haste and cut them, and then we will set out upon our journey,'

Having thus gained Huntington's permission, Pat O'Leary lost no time in repairing to the tree which he has before mentioned, where he selected two of its branches, which he thought suitable to his purposes, he quickly cut them from their parent trunk with his jacknife, and returned with them to Henry, who chose the shortest one of the two, and then said:—

'Now, Patrick, as they have all gone off and left this spot, it is time for us to follow their example.'

'Fast as yer honor plases,' replied Patrick, and so saying, he immediately followed Henry, who had advanced some paces ahead of him, and they then proceeded both together, on their intended expedition.

They walked on for some moments in silence, which, however, was broken by Henry, who thus addressed his companion,—

'Well, Patrick, what do you think of this beautiful spot?'

'Och, yer honor, and I think its just the most illigant little spot in the world, where the pratees, [meaning, possibly, the oranges and lemons,] grow on the trees, and where one never sees a snake, nor a sarpint at all, at all. Sure, and I think that the blessed Saint Patrick must have stopped at this place in the course of his travels, and killed all the snakes, and the frogs, and the vipers, bad luck to them, as he did in ould Ireland.'

'But how should you like to live here altogether?' asked Henry.

'Live, is it, master Henry? Sure, an I had rather live here than any place in the wide world, besides barrin my own blessed ould Ireland.'

'What, alone?' again asked Huntington.

'By the powers, sir, no, not a bit of it,' replied the Patlander. 'The devil a bit would Pat O'Leary wish to live alone in any place, bat I was just thinking, master Henry, that if you and Miss Hamilton, bless the light of her blessed black eyes, would only consint to be married, and live upon this pretty, convanient little island, what a nate, clane, comfortable serving man you might have in Patrick O'Leary.'

Not knowing exactly, in what way to reply to Patrick's last speech, Henry remained for the time silent, and they thus proceeded on their journey, ascending first to the top of one hill, then after passing through a fertile and beautiful valley, ascending another, until at last they got completely tired. As they reached the second valley, Henry spoke as follows:

'I think we had better rest here awhile, Patrick.'

'Just as you plase, sir,' answered his companion, 'rest or go on, it's all one to Paddy O'Leary.'

'Then I guess we will stop here,' said Henry.

So saying, he seated himself on the luxuriant green grass, beneath a fragrant orange tree, and Patrick was about to follow his example, when the sudden appearance of three men on the summit of an adjacent eminence, greeted the curious gaze which he cast around, and caused him to exclaim:

'By the powers of mud and blarney, master Henry, if there is no four legged bastes upon this illigant bit of an island, there's plenty of two legged ones.'

'What do you mean,' exclaimed Henry, starting to his feet.

'What do I mane? An sure, and what shall I mane, yer honor, except just what I said? Just look at the top of that young mountain yonder, and you will see two ugly looking two legged bastes, headed by a third, who looks for all the world like the horrid baste with 'sivin heads and ten horns,' that Father McGrave used to tell us was stabled in purgatory, and ridden by the very ould divil himself.'

Turning his eyes in the direction intimated, Henry immediately discovered the three strong men to whom Patrick had alluded, and they seemed at the same time to have seen him, for soon afterwards he observed that they were descending the hill, and walking swiftly towards the place where he and his servant were standing.

'By the boys of Bulskerry, them divils are all armed, every mother's son of them,' exclaimed O'Leary, as the strangers gained a near approach to them.

'So they are, sure enough,' answered Henry. 'But what shall we do, Pat, run away, or stop and see what they want of us?'

'It would surely be the asiest and most agreeable for both of us, to show them a light pair of heels, or, in yer honor's own words, to run away, that is, if so be that we had any where to run to,—but as we haven't, why, the best thing we can be after doing, is to—to do the best we can,—by staying where we am.'

Having arrived at this very logical, and important conclusion, our honest Hibernian flourished his shillalah above his head, but the next moment it was snatched from his grasp by Blackbeard, who cast it away to a considerable distance.

'Bad luck to yer, for a murthering blackguard,' exclaimed

Pat, as nothing daunted, he closed in with the pirate, and with his superior strength, would have easily crushed him to the earth, had not one of his (Blackbeard's) comrades struck poor Pat a violent blow on the head with the butt of his pistol, which caused him to let go his hold, and as he afterwards averred, 'knocked the life from his head down to the inds of his toes.'

Whilst this curious transaction was in progress, Henry Huntington was busily engaged in parrying the thrusts which were aimed at him by the third pirate, with his stout walking stick, (which might, perhaps, be more properly termed a heavy club,) and so lustily did he lay about him, that he soon managed to knock his adversary down, through the agency of a blow, (which, as it was afterwards discovered, fractured the villain's skull,) when Blackbeard and the other man, who had just got clear of Pat, fell suddenly upon Henry Huntington, and soon disarmed him.

This having been accomplished, Blackbeard addressed him as follows:

'Dost thou know, rash and fool-hardy man, that you have incurred death, by daring to resist my authority, and wounding one of my comrades?

'Though I know nothing either of you or your authority, or your comrades, I do know, that as far forth as I could, I have done my duty.'

'And I still have mine to do,' answered Blackbeard. 'Knowest thou that Mary Hamilton is in my power?'

'What,' exclaimed Henry, wildly, 'do I hear aright? Is my affianced in the power of—'

'If Mary Hamilton is your affianced wife, she is certainly in the power of Blackbeard, the far-famed pirate of the Roanoke.'

'God help her then,' exclaimed Henry, hardly knowing what he said.

'Amen,' exclaimed the pirate, in a tone of cruel mockery.

'If it is true, what you have told me,' said Henry, earnestly, 'only let her go, free her, Mary Hamilton, from your cruel grasp, and then you may kill, torture, do anything with my poor body that you will.'

'I shall dispose of her, and you too, just as I please,' answered Blackbeard, 'but I shall not stop longer here to bandy words with you.'

As he finished speaking, the pirate raised his silver call to his lips, and as its loud clear whistle rung out upon the still air, three more desperadoes appeared suddenly upon the scene of action, whom Blackbeard thus addressed:

'Comrades, convey this young sprig of nobility,' pointing to Henry, 'and that prostrate Irishman,' pointing to Patrick, (who was just beginning to recover from the blow which had stunned him,) 'to the cavern, under the palace, where you will see that they are closely confined.'

So saying, Blackbeard turned quickly away, and soon disappeared through the adjoining forest.

The cavern to which the pirate had alluded in his last speech, as being under the 'palace,' was a large, subterranean appartment, which was generally used by the bucaniers as a place of storage for their ill gotten plunder. This cavern had had many, and various ways of entrance, the principal one of which, was near the outside of the palace, and was opened by removing a broad, flat stone, which had been ingeniously set upright in a small banking, apparently of earth, which surrounded this singular abode.

We might as well say here, as anywhere, that we are well aware that the representation given by us of the pirate's palace and cavern, will be looked upon by many as unnatural and improbable, but when they consider that the bucaniers of that period were very numerous, and consisted of men of almost every variety of genius, which must, even in its times of relaxation, be employed about something, they will cease, perhaps, to wonder that the ingenuity of such men should be exerted in building convenient, and even elegant structures for their accommodation, and their extensive means of enriching them with ornaments the most costly, with which the numerous Indiamen they captured were freighted, will not be farther questioned.

But to return to our story.

Finding himself surrounded by four or five armed and desperate men, Huntington, concluding that resistance would be in vain, signified his readiness to follow them, whereupon he was led by two of their number to the cavern above alluded to, whilst the remaining pirates bestowed their attention upon poor Patrick O'Leary, whom, (as he had not yet recovered his powers of locomotion,) they lifted upon their shoulders and bore him away after his master, much in the same manner as they would have carried a slaughtered beast.

Having arrived with their prisoners at the place assigned for their confinement, the pirates conversed amongst themselves, as follows:

'I say, Poplin,' exclaimed one who seemed to be a kind of petty officer, 'what do you suppose our captain intends to do with these two bear cubs that we have here?'

'I cannot say, Mr. Pepper,' replied the person to whom that worthy had spoken, 'what he will do with that red-headed son of a mushroom, that lays rolled up there yonder, like a bundle of half dead lobsters, but as for the other one, he, you know, killed Pedro, and I heard the captain say that he would be hanged.'

'Then of course he will be, so that settles that affair,' replied Mr. Pepper, very coolly. 'But what do you suppose, Poplin, he is going to do with that fine lady, that he's got up overhead there?'

'Which one do you mean? He's got two of them,' said Poplin.

'Ah, yes, so he has, I recollect now. I mean both,' said Pepper.

'I cannot tell only about the youngest one,' replied Poplin, 'whom the captain is going to take on board the brig.'

'What, has the pretty little craft arrived?' asked Pepper.

'She has,' rejoined the other.

'Then its all over with the Indiaman.'

'Of course it is,' replied Poplin, significantly.

'But the Indiaman you know,' suggested Pepper, 'carried double the number of guns that the brig does.'

'She carries a Captain Rowland also,' said Poplin, drily.

'Ah, I understand it all now,' said Pepper, 'so let us confine the prisoners, and then go up and see the fun.'

So saying, a few moments afterwards, Pepper and his companions departed, leaving Henry Huntington and Pat to their own reflections.

What these reflections were, we shall leave for the present to the imagination of our readers, and resume in our next chapter the further adventures of Blackbeard, Arthur Huntington, and sweet Ellen Armstrong.

CHAPTER VI.

Interview between Blackbeard and Ellen—Attempted Murder of the latter. Interference of Elvira. Blackbeard's Departure. Elvira's History. The Escape.

After having ordered her close alongside the East Indiaman, Blackbeard immediately descended to the place where sweet Ellen Armstrong was confined as a prisoner, and addressed its occupant, in the following manner,

'So Miss Armstrong, you acted the heroine to perfection, this afternoon.'

A look of utter loathing and contempt, being the only answer which the fair Ellen deigned to bestow on the pirate's words, he continued:

'You must certainly be mad, my lovely lily of the valley, to look so scornfully upon me, who at present holds in his hand the power of thy life or death.'

'As I am well assured that you will use the awful power you speak, to put a speedy end to my wretched existence,' replied Ellen, 'I must beg of you, instantly to retire, and thus rid me of your hateful presence.'

'Stop, stop, my pretty Miss,' exclaimed Blackbeard, 'not quite so fast, if you please. In the first place you must learn, that I have at present no intention of taking your life, but on the contrary, I intend to make you my wife, as soon as circumstances will permit.'

'Pirate, fiend, villain,' exclaimed Ellen, starting up from her seat and confronting Blackbeard, with all the majesty of injured innocence, 'learn, that rather than become the wife of a desperate robber like thyself, Ellen Armstrong will die, die by her own hand, and—'

'Ha, ha ha, there you go into heroics again,' interrupted the pirate, in a tone of scornful irony, 'but I will soon find a way to bring you back to your senses. Now, listen,' he continued, after a moment's pause, and in a tone of voice changed to stern severity, 'listen I say, to my words, and mark them well. From the curious scenes which transpired awile ago on the deck of this vessel, in which you chose to act a prominent part, I could draw but one inference, and that was, that you was deeply in love with Arthur Huntington, and now I would ask of you, if this inference is correct.'

'Had you any right to put such a question to me, I should not hesitate to answer it,' replied Ellen, who by this time had attained a sort of desperate courage which enabled her to bear up under the unaccountable horrors of her situation.

'If I have not a right, you will now perceive that I have the might to compel you to answer,' exclaimed Blackbeard, who having become by this time, thoroughly infuriated, drew a poniard from his belt, and advancing, towards Ellen, who sunk pale and terrified upon her knee, at his approach, he continued:

'It is far from my wish, Miss Armstrong, to harm even a hair of your head; but you must, (and mark me, I speak not unmeaningly,) you must, I repeat, answer my question, fairly, and without equivocation. Do you love Arthur Huntington?'

Ellen shuddered, and averted her head, but answered

not. Finding his fair prisoner was not disposed to reply, Blackbeard, exclaimed with a horrid oath,

'I tell you, girl, that the pirate of the Roanoke, is not to be tampered with. Again, and for the last time, I command you to answer my question. Will you do so?'

'No,' replied Ellen firmly, 'I will not.'

'Then your blood be upon your head!' exclaimed the pirate, as springing suddenly forward, he inflicted a severe wound upon the person of sweet Ellen Armstrong, with his poniard, which caused her to fall fainting and bleeding upon the floor of the cabin.

'My God, what have I done,' muttered Blackbeard, as he gazed upon his prisoner's prostrate form.

'Murdered your sister!' exclaimed a shrill female voice, which emanated from a person who had entered the cabin unperceived, just after Ellen was wounded.

'Ha, who is that, that speaks of murder!' exclaimed the Pirate involuntarily.

'It is your mother, Elvira, who accuses you of having murdered that beautiful girl, who now lays gasping at your feet,' replied the strange female, who although she was far advanced in years, beyond the prime of life, still possessed a tall and commanding form, together with features, which, though they were somewhat wrinkled and withered, had once been pre-eminently fair and beautiful.

'Avaunt! hag,' exclaimed Blackbeard, as Elvira ceased speaking, 'begone I say, and if ever thou darest to call thyself, my mother, in my hearing, I will stab you to the very heart.'

'Am I not thy father's wife, Herbert?' replied the female.

'You say so, and it may be so,' rejoined Blackbeard, 'but at any rate you are only a social one.'

'If even that is allowed,' answered Elvira, 'you must

own that it legally puts me in your mother's place.'

'By the bones of Captain Kid, it sounds well and appropriate for you, to talk about legality,' replied Blackbeard, ironically, 'you, who hast been born and bred amongst those, who acknowledge no laws, except those of their own making. Go to, you're an idiot.'

'But I am not a murderess,' replied Elvira.

'That is more than I could swear for,' said Blackbeard.

'At least I never killed my sister,' rejoined Elvira.

'What do you mean to insinuate by that?' asked the Pirate as his muscular frame trembled with a sort of indefinable emotion.

'I mean,' replied Elvira earnestly, 'not only to insinuate, but to solemnly assert, that, that unfortunate girl, who now lies bleeding before your eyes, is your only sister.'

'What!' exclaimed Blackbeard, driven by these singular words almost to frenzy, 'Witch of Bedlam, thou liest.'

A low, faint moan, here escaped from the lips of the wounded girl, which caused Elvira, thus to address the pirate:

'Say no more at present, Herbert, I entreat you, but leave the cabin, whilst I endeavor to restore this young creature to consciousness.'

'You asserted just now, that this girl was my only sister,' replied Blackbeard, 'and before I depart I must have an explanation of your words.'

'For the love of Heaven, Herbert,' said Elvira, 'leave me alone with this maiden for the present, and to-morrow I will explain everything.'

'Upon that consideration, I will go,' avowed the pirate, 'and after which you will carefully examine her wound, and if it is likely to prove fatal, beware how you lose any time in making me aware of the fact.'

So saying, and without awaiting Elvira's reply, Blackbeard immediately left the cabin.

'Lower away the boat there,' thundered forth the pirate, as he gained the brig's quarter deck. A score or two men promptly executed this order, the boat was soon manned; Blackbeard assumed his station in the stern sheets, and was soon pulled along side of the Gladiator, whose deck he quickly reached, where he earnestly inquired of the officer in charge, for Captain Rowland.

'He went ashore, sir,' replied the man to whom he had applied, 'about one hour ago, and left orders for you to follow him at your earliest convenience.'

Upon hearing this, Blackbeard without stopping to reply, hastily re-entered his boat, and ordered his coxswain to steer directly for the shore, which he soon reached, and having landed, made the best of his way to the palace, where we will for the present leave him, whilst we look further after the fortunes of our heroine.

No sooner had the pirate, taken his departure from the cabin, than the strange female hastened to the assistance of the wounded girl, whom she supported in her arms, and then conducted her into a small but neatly furnished stateroom, which was Elvira's own apartment, where she had partly overheard the altercation which took place, as before related, between Blackbeard and Ellen, and from which she had noiselessly and unperceived entered the main cabin just after our unfortunate heroine had fallen to the floor. Here Elvira gently laid her fair charge upon her own soft couch, and proceeded immediately to examine her wound, which, although it had bled copiously, was but slight, then, after carefully dressing it, this strange woman, by the aid of appropriate restoratives soon succeeded in restoring 'sweet' Ellen Armstrong once more to consciousness.

As a confused sense of her situation began to dawn upon her mind, our heroine, after casting a wild glance around the state-room, addressed Elvira as follows:

'Good woman, for the love of Heaven, tell me where I am, and into whose hands I have fallen?'

'You are at present on board of a piratical vessel called the Fury, and in the hands of a merciless and cruel set of black-hearted villains.'

'And you,' exclaimed Ellen, hardly knowing what she said, 'how came you, a woman, to be in this horrid place?'

'That is a question,' replied Elvira 'much easier for you to ask, than it will be for me to answer, but, as some of the events connected with the sad history of my presence here, may be found to be somewhat connected with your present mysterious situation, I will lose no time in making you acquainted with the story of my past life, that is, if you think you possess strength enough to listen to the recital, which as it is to me a painful theme, I shall make as brief as possible.'

A strange and unaccountable interest in the words of the dejected being who stood before her, having taken possession of the sympathizing mind of our heroine, she signified to Elvira, that she felt strong enough to listen to any thing which might serve to explain the horrible mystery connected with her sudden captivity, and the subsequent events attendant upon it.

As Ellen finished speaking, Elvira, commenced her narration as follows:

'I was born in Lincoln, near fifty years ago. My parents were poor, but respectable trades-people, who, had they been permitted to live, until I, their only child, had reached the age of womanhood, might have, by religious counsel and strict government checked, if not wholly obliterated the reckless propensities of my passionate temper and wild, wayward disposition. But before my years had numbered ten, my parents both died within a few weeks of each other, leaving me to the care of a tyrannical old aunt, who I soon afterwards found, managed to hide, under an artful affection of religion and prudery, a base malignant and sensual character. I was immediately sent by my aunt to the parish-school, where, being naturally tractable and apt to learn I soon acquired the rudiments of a good education, and besides, I learnt also to become an expert needle-woman. No sooner did my aunt find that I was mistress of this latter accomplishment, than she took me at once from school, and compelled me to toil day and night at my needle, refusing me at the same time all necessary rest and recreation.

'Young and high-spirited as I then was, I found it impossible to bear such brutal treatment, and one day when I was about fourteen years of age, in a fit of anger and despair, I left the home of my cruel aunt, and found myself a wretched wanderer in the streets of London, without money, home, or friends. Still I wandered on, not realizing the horror of my situation, till the shades of evening began to cover the city, and the harsh knawings of cruel hunger, began inexorably to crave their natural satisfaction. Then it was that I felt myself compelled to look around for some place of shelter, but could find none, and would have returned again to my cruel aunt, but alas, all my efforts to find her habitation proved utterly fruitless, and having by this time reached the banks of the Thames, I plunged without a moment's hesitation, into its dark waters, resolving to end at once a life which promised nothing to its possessor, but wretchedness and wo. But my fatal resolution was frustrated by a man, who, unperceived had for some time previous watched my wild and desperate course, and who jumped into the water as I a second time rose to its surface, caught me by the arm, and held me tightly with one hand, whilst with the other he swam toward a small vessel, which, being but a short distance off, he managed to reach in safety.

'Having received on board this vessel every attention

which the greatest delicacy and kindness could dictate, I soon became impressed with a strong desire to become acquainted, with the character and designs of the person who had so disinterestedly preserved my life. It so happened that during a short illness which was occasioned by the cold bath I had taken in the Thames, I was assiduously attended by a female, who, as I afterwards learnt, was the wife of one of the officers of the vessel. To this woman who was very kind and attentive to my wants, I applied for the gratification of my curiosity concerning my preserver, upon which she informed me that he was a young Spaniard of good family, who commanded the vessel in which we were then situated.

'This was all I could gather from her, but a day or two afterwards I had perfectly recovered so that I could verbally thank the generous man who had saved my life, to his face. After having listened with modest though marked attention to my warm protestations of gratitude, Don Almanzor, (for such was his name,) begged me to relate to him the untoward events which had driven me to desperation and almost death.

'In accordance with his request, I gave him a brief history of my previous life, after which in view as he said, of my helpless and desolate condition, he offered to take me to his home in Cuba, where he informed me I should become an inmate of his father's family, he taking upon himself to act towards me, in every respect, the part of a friend and generous brother.

'With redoubled expressions of sincere gratitude and respect, I eagerly consented to abide by Almanzor's generous offer, and a few days afterward, the vessel in which I had so strangely become a passenger, sailed for Havana, where she arrived after a pleasant passage of three weeks.

'During the voyage, Almanzor treated me with the most delicate attention and respect, and as he was young, handsome, and unmarried, you will not be surprised when I inform you, that long before its termination, I became deeply and fervently attached to him. However, I resolved to keep my passion a secret within my own bosom, until I should know whether my affection would be reciprocated by its object, and in the mean time, I became regularly domesticated in the family of Don Almanzor, which consisted of his father, who was a rich old Spanish slave-dealer, his mother, and himself. The old people treated me in all respects, as though I had been their only daughter, and for two years I lived with them in the enjoyment of a pure and tranquil happiness, which, at the expiration of that time, was enhanced beyond measure, by an honorable offer on the part of Almanzor, of his hand and heart. As might naturally be supposed, I readily accepted an offer which agreed so well with my own inclinations, and shortly afterwards we were married, and after two more years of increased felicity had passed, I became the mother of a lovely daughter.

'My husband was at this time absent on a trading voyage, and the vessel that he was in having encountered a severe hurricane, was stranded, and every soul on board of her found a watery grave.

'This dreadful news was brought to me by Captain Rowland, who visited the island at that time, in the capacity of master of an English brig, and need I say that the horrid tidings almost drove me frantic.

'Then the insiduous tempter came, and offered me his hand, which I accepted, and thus I became what you see me now, Rowland's wife.'

'And who is this Captain Rowland?' asked Ellen, eagerly.

'He is a noted pirate,' replied Elvira.

'Did you know that when you married him?'

'I did not, if I had, sooner would I have yielded my life than united my fortune, desperate as it was, with his. When

I discovered his true character, I was his wife, on board of his vessel, and in his power, with no avenue through which I could escape, and for the sake of my child, I was forced to humble myself, and submit to his caprices.'

'Your situation must have been terrible beyond expression,' ejaculated Ellen, who had become deeply interested in the story of the unfortunate woman.

'God knows that it was so,' answered Elvira. 'The discovery of his deception came upon me suddenly, like a thunderbolt from the clouds of heaven, and I upbraided him for it in the bitterness of my heart, and he answered my reproaches at first with scornful laughter, and afterwards with a relation of the history of his past life, during which, to my utter astonishment and surprise, I learnt that he had been once before married, but that his wife had recently died, leaving two children, a son who was at that time in the vessel with his father, and an infant daughter, concerning whom, I could only then learn from Rowland, that she had been left in London, in the hands of such persons as would take good care of her.

'It was in vain after this, that I begged my cruel husband to return me and my child to Havana, he was utterly deaf to all my entreaties, although about two months after our embarcation he landed me on this desolate, but beautiful island, where, in his hours of leisure, he had with the assistance of his companions, erected and furnished with his rich but ill gotten spoils, that building which has been signified by the name of the Pirate's Palace.'

'That must be the horrid place,' exclaimed Ellen, 'which I saw this morning, and in which I fear Mary Hamilton is—is—'

'Now confined,' interrupted Elvira.

'Is it not worse than that,' exclaimed Ellen, eagerly, 'has she not met with a cruel death?'

'Oh no, that is no part of the purpose of those who have detained her,' answered Elvira.

'Do you know their true purpose, then,' asked Ellen, 'relative to her, myself, and the rest of the prisoners?'

'With regard to Miss Hamilton,' replied Elvira, 'Rowland's purpose is to force her into a union with his son.'

'And who may his son be?' again inquired Ellen.

'No other,' answered Elvira, impressively, 'but Herbert Rowland otherwise called Blackbeard, the famous pirate of the Roanoke, who is besides your only brother.'

'And Captain Rowland?'

'Is your father.'

'God of Heaven! can it be possible?' exclaimed the fair Ellen.

'It is no less possible than true,' replied Elvira.

'Then, in Heaven's name, let us free Arthur from his fetters,' exclaimed Ellen, 'and all of us escape through the cabin window into the boat, that has, I perceive, been left astern.'

Upon hearing this, Elvira immediately left the cabin, but, to Ellen's greater joy, she shortly after returned, followed by Arthur Huntington, who assisted the females into the boat, after which he entered it himself and succeeded in getting, unperceived, out of sight of the brig, upon the bosom of the wide ocean.

CHAPTER VII.

Singular Interview between Blackbeard and his Father. The Sloop-of-war. Meeting of Rowland and Henry Huntington. Life or Death. The Surprise. The Fight. The Result. Joyful Meeting. The Double Bridal. Happy Conclusion.

Upon entering the main apartment of the pirate's palace, Blackbeard encountered Captain Roderick Rowland whom he addressed as follows:

'Ha, mine honored father, so you happened to arrive here just in the nick of time to—'

'Be hung, I suppose,' muttered Rowland from between his teeth.

'Not quite so bad as that I hope,' rejoined Blackbeard.

'I hope not, too,' answered Rowland; 'but there is a very dim chance for us to escape with whole necks.'

'How so, father? What do you mean?' asked Blackbeard.

'Did not Lovelace tell you that the Fury was chased all day yesterday by one of His Majesty's sloops-of-war?'

'He did not,' replied Blackbeard, who was greatly astonished by the intelligence thus communicated. 'But what is to be done?'

'One of two things must be decided upon, and that

quickly,' answered Rowland. 'We must either get the brig underweigh, and sail for it, or else shut ourselves up here and fight for it.'

'You will be obliged to decide upon the latter position, then, for the brig is aground.'

'D—nation!' muttered Rowland, then recollecting himself, he continued:

'Well, Herbert, how many of our crew is there now about the palace?'

'Not more than a dozen.'

'There should be thirteen, I think,' replied Rowland.

'And there probably would have been had not one of them had his brains knocked out this morning in a scuffle with one of your passengers.'

'Which one of them was it who dared to strike one of us?' asked Rowland.

'A devilish rum one, I can tell you, father. If I mistake not, his name was Henry Huntington.'

'Have you got him in custody?'

'Ay, he is safely confined in the cavern.'

'And I hope we shall have an opportunity to hang him,' exclaimed Rowland. 'And Mary Hamilton, is she too, safe?'

'She is, I believe, in the next room with Violette,' answered Blackbeard.

'Herbert, I have resolved that you shall marry that girl,' said Rowland abruptly.

'Hell and fury!' exclaimed Blackbeard. 'I did not expect that. In your letter, written to me from London, you stated that I was to marry one of the two girls who were about to take passage with you in the Gladiator, so I concluded you meant the youngest, and I have made love to her accordingly.'

'Good God, Herbert, she is your only sister!'

'Then I have killed her!'

'How?' exclaimed Rowland.

'I have murdered her,' replied Blackbeard, who then related to his father the conversation that had passed between himself and Ellen, and its terrible result.

'I little thought,' said Rowland, as Blackbeard finished speaking, 'that I was training you up to outvie myself in villany. Are you sure she is dead?'

'I hope she is,' replied Blackbeard, ironically.

'Beware then!' exclaimed Blackbeard; 'for if she has gone, if her pure spirit has departed, you shall soon follow her.'

'If I follow her I shall be sure of Heaven, then, which would by no means be the case if I followed you in your exit from the world,' muttered Blackbeard.

'Why, Herbert,' exclaimed Rowland, 'you will soon arrive to be the very prince of bucaniers, if your career is not cut short by a—'

'Halter,' interrupted Blackbeard. 'Well, if it is, I shall not have to swing alone—there is some consolation in that—there is nothing like plenty of company, whichever road we may be travelling.'

'Ha! ha! ha!' laughed Rowland. 'You're a sad dog, Herbert, and well worthy the lineage from which you have descended. Now you will go and order the men to get their arms in readiness for a desperate fight, and despatch two of them to the brig with orders for her crew to hasten to our assistance.'

'But what shall be done with the passengers and crew of the Indiaman,' asked Blackbeard.

'There are none there of any great consequence to us,' answered Rowland, 'and as there is no room for us to be cumbered with them here, we shall be obliged to let them run a chance of escape. You can also tell Pepper to bring the prisoners now in the cavern immediately into my presence.'

Having received the above orders, Blackbeard departed upon his errand, and soon after, Pepper entered Rowland's presence, followed by Henry Huntington and his faithful servant, Mr. Patrick O'Leary.

After surveying the two prisoners for some moments in silence, Rowland spoke to Huntingdon in the following manner:

'You are undoubtedly much surprised at meeting me in this place, are you not, Mr. Huntington?'

'Since the mysterious events of this morning I have ceased to be surprised at anything,' answered Henry.

This reply was apparently unheeded by Rowland, who thus continued:

'I have sent for you here in order to inform you that to-morrow will be the last day of your existence. You have forfeited your life in two several and different ways to the laws of the free sons of the ocean.'

Here Rowland paused for a reply; but as Henry did not choose to make any, he continued:

'When you considered me to be nothing but the master of a paltry Indiaman, you treated me with haughtiness, contempt, and scorn that I never did forgive, and never shall.'

'You was treated by me, as in my estimation, you deserved to be,' replied Henry, boldly.

'Very well,' answered Rowland, as a sardonic grin illuminated his flexible countenance, 'as you are self-condemned on that charge, there is no occasion for me to bring forward the others, so to-morrow morning you die!'

'Oh! say not so, but recall your cruel words!' exclaimed Mary Hamilton, as she rushed into Rowland's presence from the inner apartment.

'Ha! who have we here?' exclaimed Rowland, as the wild tones of Mary's voice fell upon his ear.

'You see before you, sir,' replied Miss Hamilton, 'a poor unfortunate girl who only claims from you the boon of her friend's life.'

'You plead in vain, Miss Hamilton,' answered Rowland, coldly, 'his life has been twice forfeited, and were an angel from Heaven to ask it, it would avail nothing—he must and shall die.'

'Then will I die with him!'

'Ha! sits the wind in that quarter,' muttered Rowland in a low tone, then raising his voice, and addressing Mary, he said:

'I suppose then, I am to infer that you are in love with this Mr. Huntington.'

'You must infer what you please, sir,' replied Mary, 'I shall say no more.'

'I must speak myself, then,' replied Rowland. 'Now Miss Hamilton, hear me. Some ten years have elapsed since I first become acquainted with your father in Rio, where I had landed to dispose of a cargo of negroes. I also soon became acquainted with the vast extent of his wealth, with the fact that, upon the event of his death, it would fall into your hands, and from that hour I resolved that you should marry my son. To bring about this result I have practised every art which my inventive genius could suggest in order to get you in my power, and after finding out where and with whom you resided, I have watched day and night for an opportunity to secure your person, and at last success crowned my efforts, as I obtained the command of the vessel in which, as I was well assured beforehand, you took passage for the purpose of joining your father. Now my son is here, and you, his destined bride, we have a regularly educated Roman priest here also, who can legally solemnize the marriage rites; therefore consent to wed my son, Herbert Rowland, and the life of Henry Huntington is saved.'

For some moments after the conclusion of Rowland's speech, Mary uttered not a word, but stood with uplifted eyes, as if in silent suppication to Heaven for guidance in this her hour of peril and danger.

The solemn silence which reigned in the apartment was soon broken by Rowland who thus again addressed Miss Hamilton:

'Will you consent to become my son's wife?'

'Never!' replied the fair girl, firmly. 'Although the life of my friend is dearer to me than my own, I will never consent to save it by a dishonored allegiance with the son of a pirate.'

'Then an angel spoke,' exclaimed Henry.

'By the piper that played before Moses, and I can swear on the blissed book to that same, masther Henry,' ejaculated Pat O'Leary, who, with a countenance swaying alternately from laughing to crying, formed a somewhat ludicrous contrast to the rest of the group.

'Take that young sprig of nobility below again, Pepper,' exclaimed Rowland.

As Henry was about to follow the individual in question, who was preparing to depart with his prisoner, Mary said:

'Farewell, Henry, be of good cheer, and despair not, for He who tempers the wind to the shorn lamb, will most assuredly deliver you from your villanous persecutor.'

Having thus spoken, Miss Hamilton immediately retired into the adjoining apartment.

'Come, young man,' exclaimed Pepper, 'bear a hand, and trot here in my wake.'

'Lead on,' answered Henry, and so saying he followed

Pepper towards the door.

They had hardly reached it, however, before their farther progress was impeded by the entrance of Blackbeard, who almost breathlessly exclaimed:

'It is all over with us, father. The boats from the sloop-of-war on the other side of the island, and their crews armed to the teeth, are now within a few rods of the palace.'

'Be the bones of St. Patrick, an' sure that is the most illegant news that iver graated the ears iv a jintleman in disthress!' exclaimed Pat O'Leary, who was in an ecstacy of joy at the prospect of his speedy deliverance.

'What is to be done, father?' asked Blackbeard.

'Done,' exclaimed Rowland, in a voice of thunder, 'why, we must fight and die, as we have lived, at war with all mankind.'

By this time a considerable number of the pirates had entered the palace, and were ordered by Rowland to close the doors and barricade them with whatever moveables they could find, but before his command could be executed, the apartment was forcibly entered by the crew of one of the launches of His Majesty's sloop of war, Vengeance, headed by an officer, who called out to the inmates,—

'Surrender in the name of King George!'

'In the name of King Lucifer, then, I will never surrender,' exclaimed Rowland, as he aimed a blow at the officer with his cutlass.

The fight thus began, and soon became general, but although the pirates fought desperately, they were soon overpowered by the superior numbers and coolness of their adversaries, and as a pistol shot laid Rowland upon the floor, the few desperadoes who remained, agreed to surrender at discretion, with the exception of Blackbeard, who fought like a tiger, until he fell covered with wounds by his father's side, the red current of life mingling with that of his unnatural parent.

'Some one must have betrayed us, Herbert,' exclaimed the now dying Rowland, 'and the curse of,—but no, Clarice, I cannot come to thee, thou art in Heaven. O God, my child, my dearest one, where art thou, Clarice, Elvira, El—'

Here the sound of his voice was heard no more. Rowland was dead!

As his cold hand fell lifeless by his side, it rested upon the cold clammy cheek of his son, and it became evident to all around that the short but eventful career of Blackbeard, the far-famed Pirate of Roanoke was forever ended.

Although the Fury had managed to outsail the sloop-of-war, on the day previous to the events above related, the captain of the latter, well knowing that the island of Trinidad had long been a piratical rendezvous, naturally supposed that the brig would stop there, and as he made the land just before night-fall he determined the next day to explore the island, hoping that he might thereby be enabled to trace the desperadoes to their lurking-place.

The wind changing during the night, brought the Vengeance, next morning, some few miles to the leeward of the island, on the side opposite from that where the Fury had grounded, so that it was late in the afternoon before she could get near enough to lower her boats.

Just before, however, the order was given to embark the several boat's crews, the man on the look-out exclaimed:

'There is something close alongside here, which looks like a boat.'

The captain of the Vengeance, upon going forward to see what the strange thing might be, was greatly astonished at being hailed as follows:

'Ship ahoy. For the love of Heaven stop and take on board two helpless women, who have but just escaped from the pirates.'

This request was speedily acceded to, the sails of the Vengeance were hove aback, and the next moment Arthur Huntington, accompanied by Ellen Armstrong and the pirate's wife, were safe upon her deck, where the former lost no time in making the captain of the Vengeance acquainted with the events which had that day transpired, whilst Elvira volunteered to direct the officer who had been entrusted with the command of the boats, to the pirate's palace, which otherwise he might not have found.

Before midnight, the whole party who had landed upon the island in the morning, met each other once again, upon the deck of the Vengeance, and many and sincere were the thanks they returned to Heaven for their deliverance out of the murderous hands of the pirate of the Roanoke.

Five years after the occurrence of the singular events above narrated, the mansion of Lord Armstrong, situated near the mouth of the Roanoke river, in the province of North Carolina, was brilliantly illuminated, as if for a season of great rejoicing. And such indeed was the fact. Soon after night-fall a gay party had assembled in the earl's parlor, and shortly afterwards entered Henry Huntington, holding by the hand the fair and stately Mary Hamilton, immediately followed by his brother Arthur and sweet Ellen Armstrong, the whole party being succeeded by a clergyman, attired in the sacerdotal robes of the church of Rome.

That night, dear reader, witnessed the consummation of a double bridal.

Elvira, the pirate's wife, and her daughter Violette, were present at the wedding, and so was Misther Pat O'Leary, who afterwards declared that 'by the powers of mud, it was indade the pleasantest night he had iver passed in his life, so it was.'

Kind reader, it only remains for us to say that the descendants of Arthur and Henry Huntington still continue to reside upon the pleasant banks of the Roanoke, and often take great pleasure in recounting to each other the exploits of the far-famed Blackbeard, and the providential and almost miraculous escape of their ancestors from the blood-stained hands of Herbert and Roderick Rowland.

THE END.